Piano • Vocal

Saturday Night

Music and Lyrics by Stephen Sondheim

Book by Julius J. Epstein

Music Editor: Paul McKibbins
Front Cover Photo: Harold Roth

SATURDAY NIGHT is represented through special arrangement by
Music Theatre International, 421 West 54th Street, New York, NY 10019

ISBN 978-0-7935-9576-1

HAL•LEONARD®
CORPORATION
7777 W. BLUEMOUND RD. P.O. BOX 13819 MILWAUKEE, WI 53213

Visit Hal Leonard Online at
www.halleonard.com

SATURDAY NIGHT

A Brief History of the Show

Saturday Night was to have been Stephen Sondheim's professional debut. Julius J. and Philip G. Epstein, twin Hollywood screenwriters who had won an Academy Award for *Casablanca*, had written a play entitled *Front Porch in Flatbush*. (It was their last collaboration before Philip's death.) It was set in 1929 and was about their third brother and a group of young people in Brooklyn investing in the stock market.

Lemuel Ayers, designer of *Oklahoma!* and co-producer of *Kiss Me, Kate*, believed it was ideal material for a musical and was keen to produce the piece. He and Julius Epstein invited Stephen Sondheim to write music and lyrics. Backers' auditions were underway in 1954 and *The New York Times* reported the confirmed plans for the production. But when Ayers died suddenly, the project was halted.

Subsequent plans for Ayers' widow to produce the show never came to fruition. In 1959 Jule Styne, Sondheim's collaborator on *Gypsy*, became smitten with *Saturday Night*. He hoped to produce it, with Bob Fosse both directing and playing the role of Gene. Again *The New York Times* prematurely heralded these now official plans for the production in June, 1959. During the auditions, Sondheim decided that he did not wish to proceed with an old project and wanted to go on to new work.

Thirty-six years later, students at the University of Birmingham (England) presented excerpts of the never-performed show in a concert version at The Bridewell Theatre Company in London. The concert was attended by the composer himself. During a question-and-answer session after the concert, Sondheim was asked if he would allow the Bridewell company to present the first full production of *Saturday Night*. With the composer's blessing, plans were launched, and the 1954 musical finally opened on December 11, 1997. A subsequent recording of the show, based on the Bridewell production, was released on First Night Records. The authors presented a revised edition of the show for the American premiere by the Pegasus Players in Chicago on May 19, 1999.

SATURDAY NIGHT

Contents

Discography of Songs

Saturday Night (complete show), original Bridewell cast (1998, First Night Records)

All for You
Recording: Unsung Sondheim (1993, performed by Davis Gaines)

In the Movies
Recording: Unsung Sondheim (1993, performed by Marilyn Cooper)

Isn't It?
Recording: Myrra Malmberg: What Can You Lose? (1996); A Stephen Sondheim Evening (1983, performed by Victoria Mallory)

That Kind of a Neighborhood
Recording: A Stephen Sondheim Evening (1983, excerpt entitled "Fair Brooklyn")

Love's a Bond
Recording: Unsung Sondheim (1993, performed by Walter Willison)

A Moment with You
Recording: Marry Me a Little (1981, performed by Craig Lucas, Suzanne Henry)

Saturday Night
Recordings: Unsung Sondheim (1993, performed by Stan Chandler, David Engel, Larry Rabern, Guy Stroman); A Stephen Sondheim Evening (1983); Marry Me a Little (1981, performed by Craig Lucas, Suzanne Henry)

So Many People
Recordings: Myrra Malmberg: What Can You Lose? (1996); Mandy Pantinkin: Experiment (1994); Meg Mackay: So Many People (1994); A Collector's Sondheim (1985, performed by Craig Lucas, Suzanne Henry); Jackie Cain & Roy Kral: Sondheim (1982); Marry Me a Little (1981, performed by Craig Lucas, Suzanne Henry); Richard Rodney Bennett: A Different Side of Sondheim (1979); Sondheim: A Musical Tribute (1973; performed by Susan Browning, Jack Cassidy)

What More Do I Need?
Recordings: Dawn Upshaw: I Wish It So (1994); A Collector's Sondheim (1985, performed by Liz Callaway); A Stephen Sondheim Evening (1983, performed by Liz Callaway); The Other Side of Sondheim (1988, performed by Jane Harvey)

The Story

The story of *Saturday Night* takes place in the Spring of 1929, and is told over three consecutive Saturday evenings. A group of male friends in their early twenties are sitting on the front porch of a house in Brooklyn. They commiserate about not having dates ("Saturday Night"). Gene Gorman enters, dressed in tails and ready to crash the Junior League Cotillion at the Plaza Hotel in Manhattan ("Class"). Gene, a runner on Wall Street, asks his pals for $100 each to buy some hot stock. He promises them that they'll all be rich within a week. Gene's cousin is heading to Florida and asks Gene to look after his fancy car, a Pierce-Arrow. A female friend's sister and her friend enter and the guys argue over what the couplings will be as they head to a movie ("Delighted, I'm Sure").

Gene arrives at the Plaza (the band singer is singing "Love's a Bond") and as luck would have it, he meets Helen, a girl who is also crashing the party by pretending to be a southern aristocrat. The two pair up ("Isn't It?"). The scene shifts to a movie theater, where the guys and girls from the porch scene have gone ("In the Movies"). Late that night, back on the front porch in Brooklyn, everyone has gathered. Helen calls on the phone for Gene, and asks if she can come over. Bobby explains to his friends the art of seduction ("Exhibit A"). Helen arrives and admits that she's really from Brooklyn and isn't a southern aristocrat after all. Gene doesn't care, and he and Helen dance to a romantic song on a record ("A Moment with You"). He takes Helen to see an upscale apartment for rent, and he leases the flat, convinced he'll make it big in the stock market gamble.

The next Saturday night comes along. Gene is broke. The stock scheme is collapsing ("Montana Chem."). He rashly sells his absent cousin's car. Even though Helen hates what he's done, she admits she loves Gene ("So Many People"). The whole gang sings "One Wonderful Day" in anticipation of Gene and Helen's wedding, with Bobby demurring.

Act Two begins with the third Saturday night. Gene is being hounded by police detectives and the rental agent. The cousin and owner of the sold car arrives back in town, and as fate or musical comedy would have it, he is also named Eugene Gorman. Mistaking him for the Gene who went off with his friends' money, is involved in a shady stock deal, who sold his friend's car and is not honoring an apartment lease, the detectives take him to the police station. Meanwhile, Gene's married friends Hank and Celeste remember their first date ("I Remember That"). Gene and Helen try to have a good time on the town together ("All for You"). A serious quarrel develops, and Gene leaves.

At the police station, the gang sings about helping Gene out ("That Kind of a Neighborhood"). The identity confusion between the two Genes is cleared up. Helen offers Gene a job at her father's business (plucking chickens). Helen says how content she is with her life in Brooklyn after all ("What More Do I Need?"). A happy reprise ends the show on a high note.

Saturday Night

from the Musical **SATURDAY NIGHT**

Music and Lyrics by
STEPHEN SONDHEIM

Brightly ♩=112

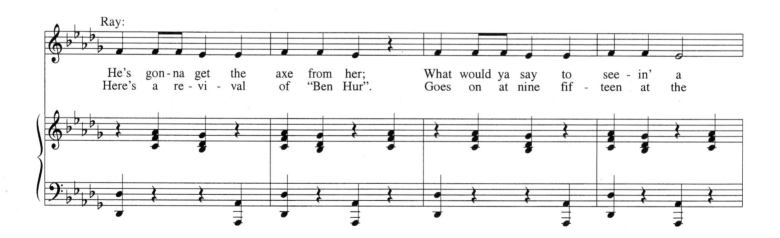

Ray:

He's gon-na get the axe from her; What would ya say to see-in' a
Here's a re-vi-val of "Ben Hur". Goes on at nine fif - teen at the

I've got - ta spend an - oth - er Sat - ur - day night____ At home with the
I got my bud - dies and my bud - dies are fine____ But not on a

Sun - day Times.____
Sat - ur - day night!____

staccato

To Coda ⊕

Ted:

Moon - light on Flat - bush A - ve - nue That's what I call a love - ly view.____

mp

Tempo I

f

Poco meno mosso

Dino:
(2nd time)

Easy

So

rall.

mp

what can you do on a Sat - ur - day night a - lone?_____

Who needs a view on a Sat - ur - day night a - lone?_____

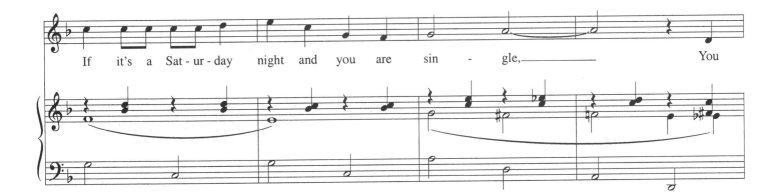

If it's a Sat - ur - day night and you are sin - gle,_____ You

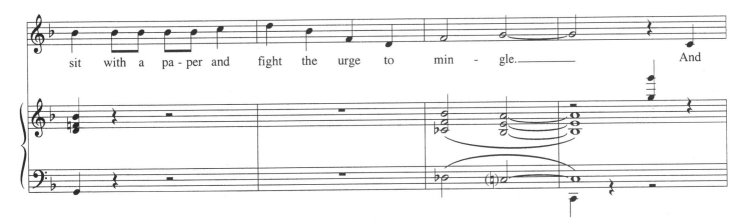

sit with a pa - per and fight the urge to min - gle._____ And

home is a place where you got - ta go back a - lone._____

If it's a Sat-ur-day night and you are sin-gle,_____ You

If it's a Sat-ur-day sin - gle,_____ You

a - lone? Sin - gle,_____ You

Sat-ur-day night a - lone? Sin - gle,_____ You

sit with a pa-per and fight the urge to min - gle._____ And

sit with a pa-per and fight the urge to min - gle._____

sit with a pa-per and fight the urge to min - gle._____

sit with a pa-per and fight the urge to min - gle.

Thing's-'d be diff-'rent an-y oth-er night in-stead,— But we're on our own on a

Thing's-'d be diff-'rent an-y oth-er night in-stead,— But we're on our own on a

lone. Diff-'rent an-y oth-er night in-stead,— But we're on our own on a

thing's-'d be diff-'rent an-y oth-er night in-stead,— But we're on our own on a

mf

All:

Sat-ur-day night,— With no one to phone on a Sat-ur-day night,—

— And when you're a-lone on a Sat-ur-day night,—

cresc.

You might as well be dead!

(Orchestra)

f

ff *detache*

Dino:
(with his elbow)

Class

from the Musical **SATURDAY NIGHT**

Music and Lyrics by
STEPHEN SONDHEIM

sell; It's— the Pla - za Ho - tel!_____ I'm

cross-ing the rain - bow,_____ I'm tak-ing a ride_____ To a

raz - zle daz - zle world_ On_ the oth - er side._____ Ver - y spe - cial

world. Got - ta have a pass_____ called

A bit brighter, with bounce

"Class." _____ A man can be___ A run-ner by day,___ But

so - cial - ly, What counts___ is the way___ He looks.

That's what I mean___ by___ Class. I've got two suits,___ Just

two to my name, I've got just two suits, But both___ of 'em came From Brooks.

leggiero

That's what I mean— by— Class.

Class is when you're wrapped— in Har - ris tweed And al - ways look im-pec - ca - ble in—

— what— you're wrapped in. Class is when you dem - on-strate your breed - ing,

Like for in - stance when you call a wait - er "Cap - tain." This— is why—— A

room is a "flat."_ You don't say "tie," You call___ it "cra - vat."_

Say you drink_from a "tum - bler" in - stead of a glass._

That's the mark of some - one who has what I call Class.

dim.

Interlude

A bit brighter, with bounce

The beau - ti - ful peo - ple_ who

mp *legato*

Now tell__ me,__ what's wrong with that?_____

Ted:

The beau - ti - ful peo - ple__ are not for you;__ Their

blood is blue.__ They're out of your class. Be your - self,__ Gene,

Be your - self.__ Be your - self,__ Gene, Be your self.__

(Voices continue under)

Gene:
I'd like to own a Rolls Royce, A Braque, A Du - fy.

All things ex - pen - sive and choice And

rare. I've got the

friends that I need To share them with me, But I need the things to

share._____ Some peo - ple

live out their lives_____ And don't give a damn._____

They buy_____ things on the in - stall - ment plan._____

___ That's not_____ for me; I don't want_____ to

be what I am;— I want to be what I can!——

—— The beau - ti - ful peo - ple—— get up at noon—— And

mf

spend all their time— hav-ing fun.—— They bet - ter make way— 'Cause

cresc. *f*

ve - ry soon The Four—— Hun - dred will be Four Hun - dred and—

L.H.

R.H.

Mis - sus du - Pont, You say to her, "Oui, nat - ur-elle - ment, Ma'm -

selle!" That's what I mean by__ Class.

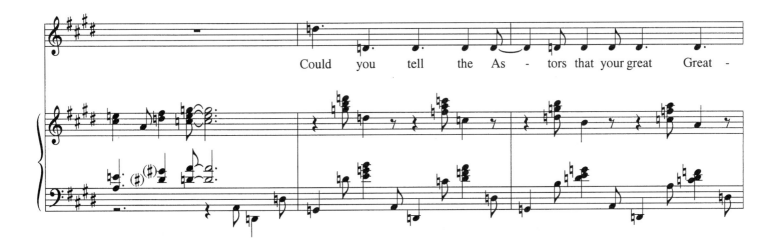

Could you tell the As - tors that your great Great -

Celeste:

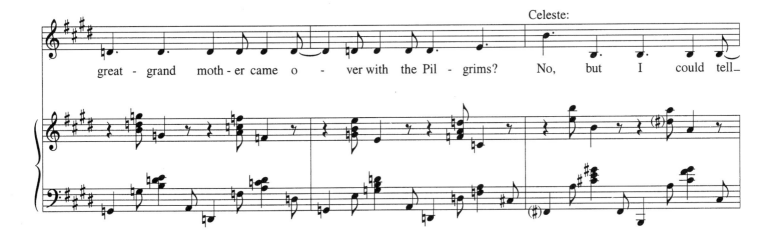

great - grand moth - er came o - - ver with the Pil - grims? No, but I could tell__

Delighted, I'm Sure

from the Musical **SATURDAY NIGHT**

Music and Lyrics by
STEPHEN SONDHEIM

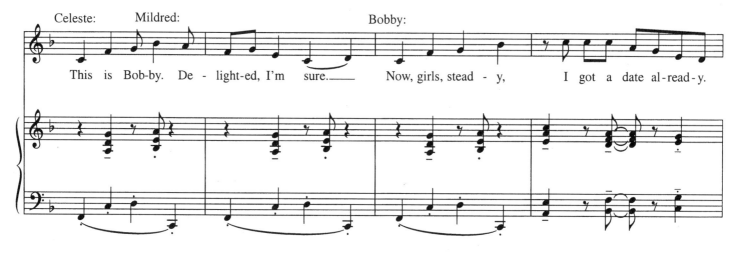

This is Bob-by. De - light-ed, I'm sure.____ Now, girls, stead - y, I got a date al-read-y.

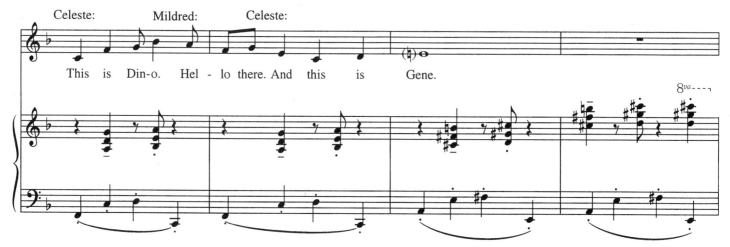

This is Din-o. Hel - lo there. And this is Gene.

Ooh, my good - ness Like from a mag - a - zine...____

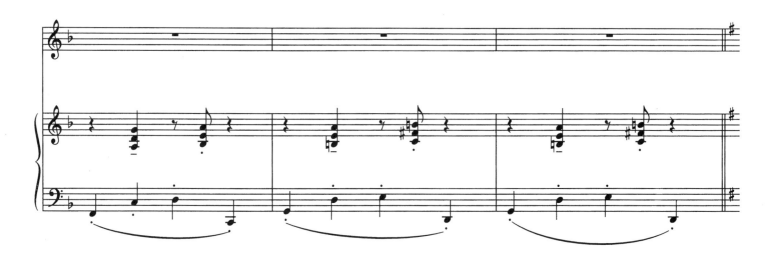

Love's A Bond

from the Musical **SATURDAY NIGHT**

Music and Lyrics by
STEPHEN SONDHEIM

When put— to the test, I like— to in - vest,

But I won't be a great— fin - an - cier———— Love's the

stock I like;———— It's free and clear. And it - 'll be

blue - chip if you chip in with me, my dear!————

Refrain

Love's a bond that's pure,_____ It's di - vi - dends are sure._____ This bond if you get_____ it, Is sta - ble and yet_____ it Will grow if you let_____ it Ma - ture. And

marcato

dar - ling, have you heard?_____ The

mar - ket's spi - ral - ling like a bird._____ As

A. T. and T._____ will Go up and up, we_____ will, 'Cause

this new love of ours is gilt - edged pre - ferred._____

Love's a bond that's pure,_____ It's di - vi -

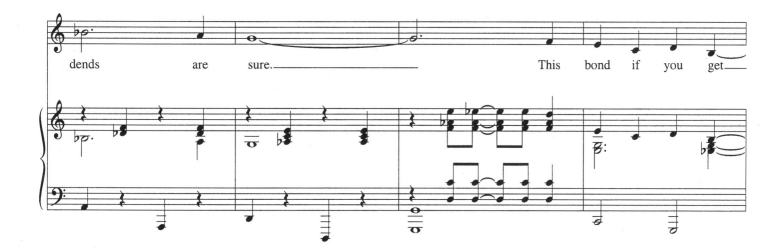

dends are sure._____ This bond if you get_____

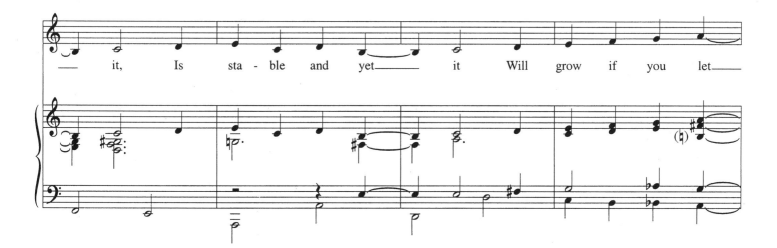

_____ it, Is sta - ble and yet_____ it Will grow if you let_____

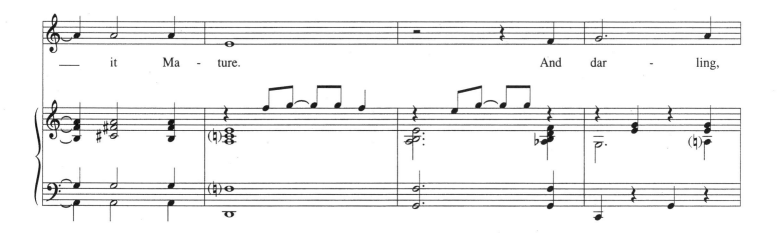

_____ it Ma - ture. And dar - ling,

have you heard?_____ A rise in stocks_

_ has just oc - curred._____ If sold in the dark,_

_ it Will soon flood the mar - ket. 'Though love is

com - mon, still and all,_ it's pre - ferred._____

Isn't It?

from the Musical **SATURDAY NIGHT**

Music and Lyrics by
STEPHEN SONDHEIM

We're so right, Are - n't we? I mean, for

danc - ing. Hold me

tight, Cling to me — I mean, my hand. _____

cresc.

I feel fine. I'm a -

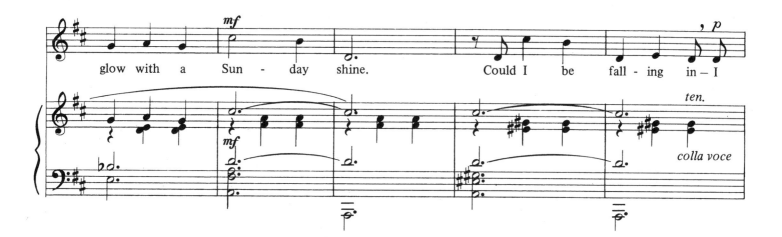

glow with a Sun - day shine. Could I be fall - ing in – I

mean _____ to say, _____ Well, an - y - way, Is - n't it

grand? _____

In The Movies

from the Musical **SATURDAY NIGHT**

Music and Lyrics by
STEPHEN SONDHEIM

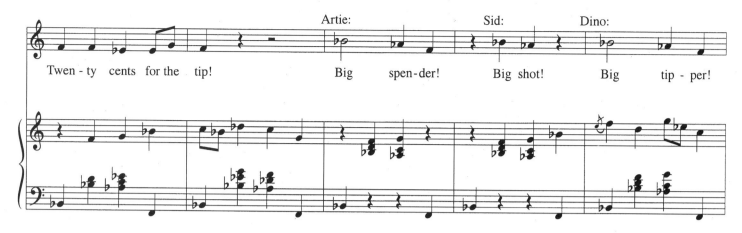

Twen - ty cents for the tip!   **Artie:** Big spen-der!   **Sid:** Big shot!   **Dino:** Big tip - per!

(Dialogue)

Hank:
I paid fif - ty cents for the hat - check. Fif - ty cents for the

hat - check.   **Sid:** I did-n't wear an - y hat!   **Hank:** So

Artie:
I did-n't wear an - y hat, So we don't have to pay for the hat - check.

Slower ♩=84
(GIRLS enter)

Tempo I
Dino: Sid: Hank:
I paid! I paid! And don't for-get the Her-shey bars!

Tempo II
Laura: Clara:
Stel - la Dal - las had her dreams. She would see her

Laura:

daugh-ter dwell in state-ly homes and pal - a - ces. Stel - la went to

Mildred:

all ex - tremes, And fin - al - ly a wealth-y fel - la showed at Stel - la

Celeste:

Dal - las - 's. Stel - la worked it pret - ty well, But in the last an -

ten. Trio:

al - y - sis, Though Stel-la's daugh-ter got the swell, All Stel - la got was cal - lus - es. It

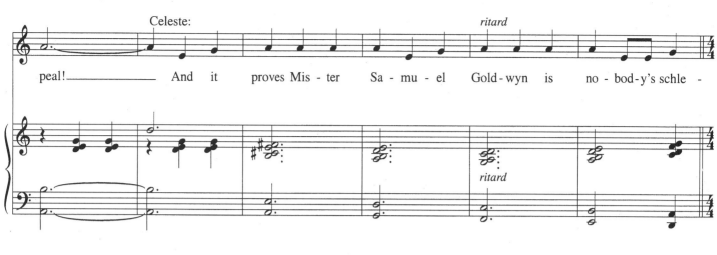

Celeste:

peal!_____ And it proves Mis-ter Sa-mu-el Gold-wyn is no-bod-y's schle-

Allegro ma non troppo ♩=136

miel. If a

mf risoluto

per-son—treads the path of sin So her daugh-ter— can eat quail,_____ In the

mov-ies—she's a he-ro-ine, But in Brook-lyn she'd go to jail._____ In the

Tempo primo

dream.

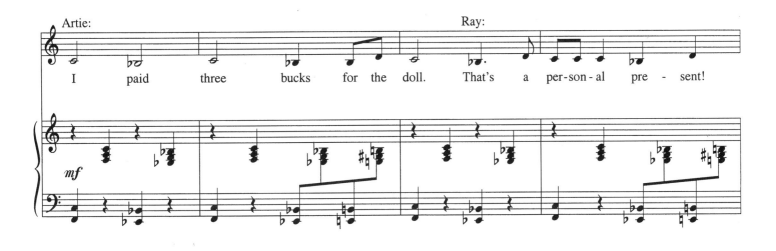

Artie: I paid three bucks for the doll. Ray: That's a per-son-al pre - sent!

Ted: Mil-dred's your date! Dino: Mil-dred's your date! Artie: Mil-dred's our col - lec - tive date! We

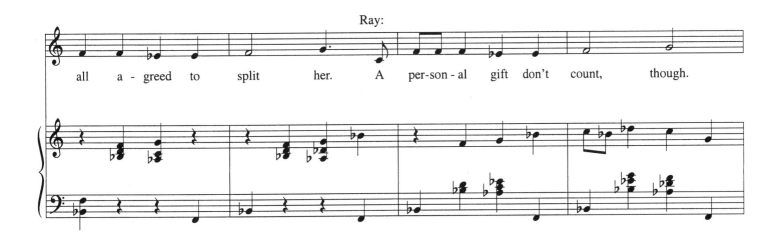

all a - greed to split her. Ray: A per-son-al gift don't count, though.

Artie:
Split three bucks four ways, You and me and Ted and Di - no! It on-ly cost two for

Ray:

all that we know!

(Dialogue)

Girls (spoken):

Look what's com-ing: Val - en - ti - no!

ritard

Slowly, mysteriously ♩=52

Clara:

Val - en - ti - no,_____

Laura:

Vil - ma

Bank - y,_____ Lots of sand and_____ hank - y

Mildred:

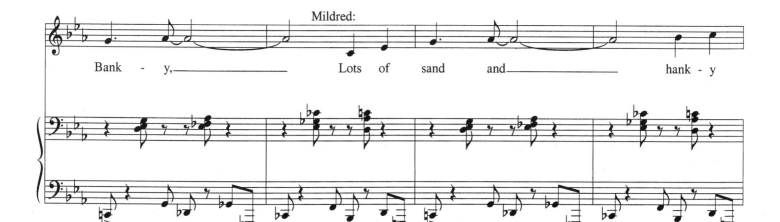

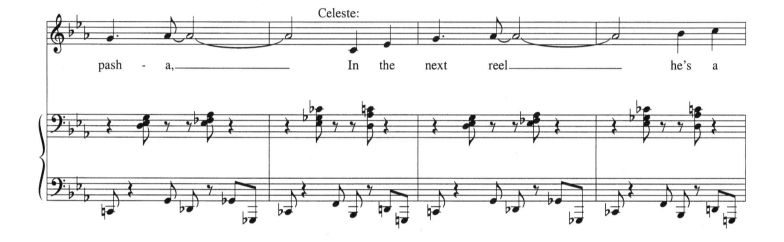

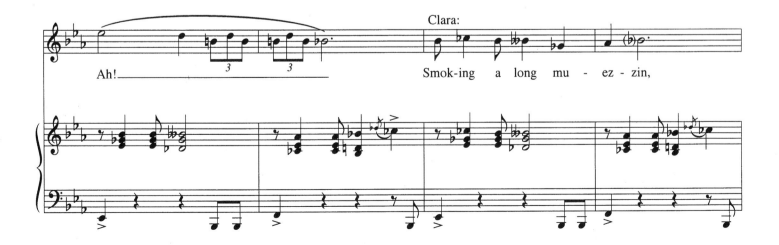

Celeste:

Wear-ing a pur-ple tur-ban,_____ When-ev-er he smokes, He half-shuts his eyes. So

may-be some spies Filled it with Bour-bon. Trio: Ah!_____

Celeste:

_____ Hey, wake up, there,_____ The-da

Ba-ra,_____ You're a long way_____ from the Sa-

fold my tent And pay the rent And leave the vamp-ing to the vamps._____

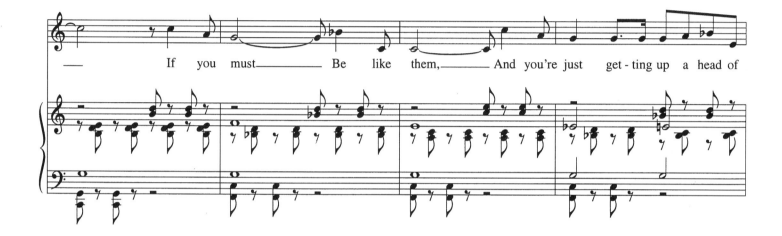

_____ If you must_____ Be like them,_____ And you're just get-ting up a head of

steam,_____ Nev - er trust_____ M - G - M! Hold your hips in and set-tle for the

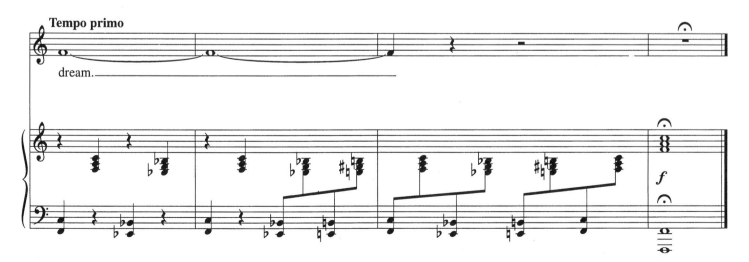

Tempo primo

dream._____

Exhibit "A"

from the Musical **SATURDAY NIGHT**

Music and Lyrics by
STEPHEN SONDHEIM

loor.   To im - press,   To ap - peal   Use fin-

esse,   Be gen - teel._____

Ex-hib - it "A":   A
Ex-hib - it "E":   A

couch   must   be   sprayed   with   the   fra - grance   of
flask   is   for   girls   who   may   have   their   sus-

new pine, And soon all ver-ti-cal things-'ll be su - pine.___ A
pi - cions. A shot will help 'em for-get in-hi-bi - tions.___ The

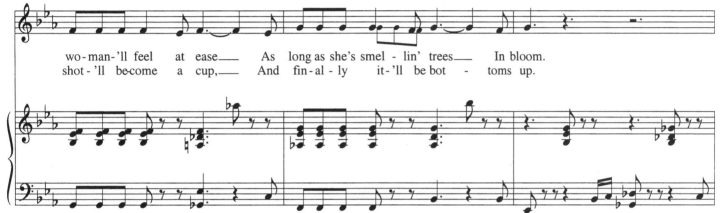

wo-man-'ll feel at ease___ As long as she's smel-lin' trees___ In bloom.
shot-'ll be-come a cup,___ And fin-al-ly it-'ll be bot - toms up.

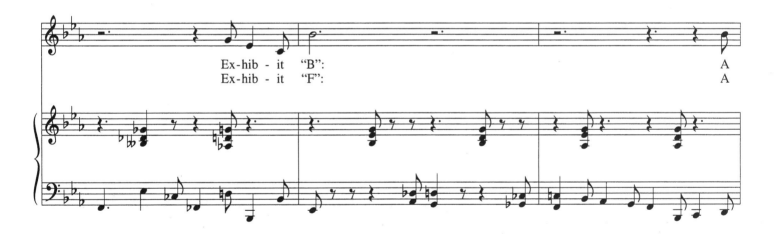

Ex-hib - it "B": A
Ex-hib - it "F": A

door ain't a door till you close it and
ham - mock is draft - y, A place to catch

lock it. She can't get out if the key's in your pock - et,_____ And
cold in. But just re - mem - ber that si - lence is gold - en,_____ And

no - bod - y else but you can get in_____ the room!
ham - mocks are bet - ter than so - fas or swings: No springs!

Ex - hib - it "C":
Ex - hib - it "G":

Mu - sic,_____ if it's slow and smooth, Hath charms to soothe The
Lights_____ make a room cheer - i - er, But I pre - fer The

D.S. al Coda

Coda

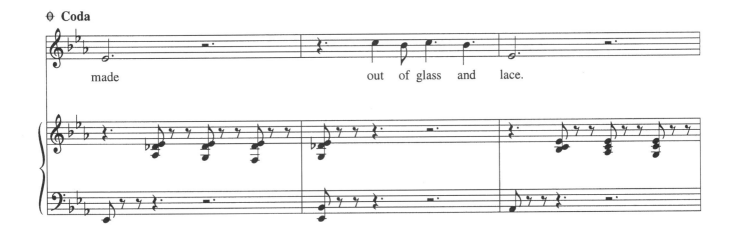

made   out of glass and lace.

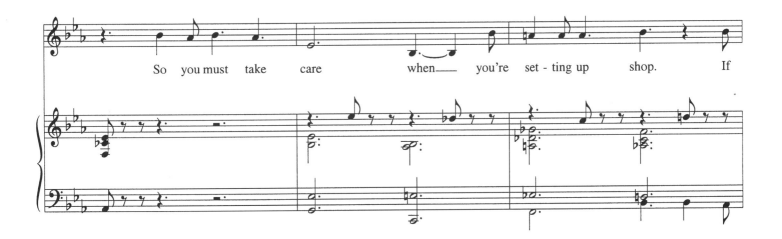

So you must take care   when___ you're set - ting up   shop.   If

you   want___ to come out on   top,   Then put   ev - 'ry

prop in its prop - er place. Just check - ing: —

A, B, C, D, E, F,

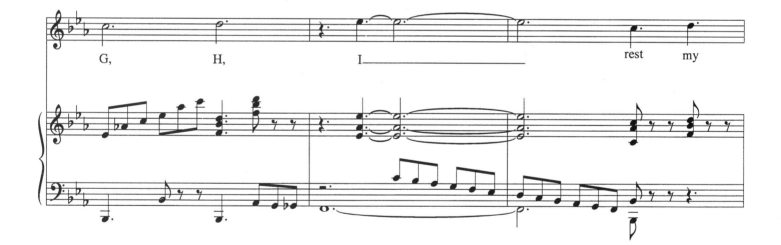

G, H, I _____ rest my

case!

A Moment With You

from the Musical **SATURDAY NIGHT**

Music and Lyrics by
STEPHEN SONDHEIM

look _____ in your eyes was a plea - sure, My

look _____ in your eyes was a plea - sure, My

p

cresc. poco a poco

per - son-al trea - sure was in it. _____

per - son-al trea - sure was in it. _____

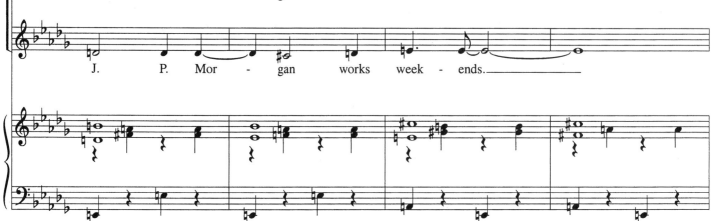

J. P. Mor - gan works week - ends. _____

J. P. Mor - gan works week - ends. _____

I'm_____ ov - er - joyed!_____

I'm no more__ in a void, My cares_ are de -

__ I a - void be - ing low_____ Just by

stroyed, I a - void be - ing low_____ Just by

D.S. al Coda

spend - ing a mo - ment with you!_____ It

spend - ing a mo - ment with

Coda

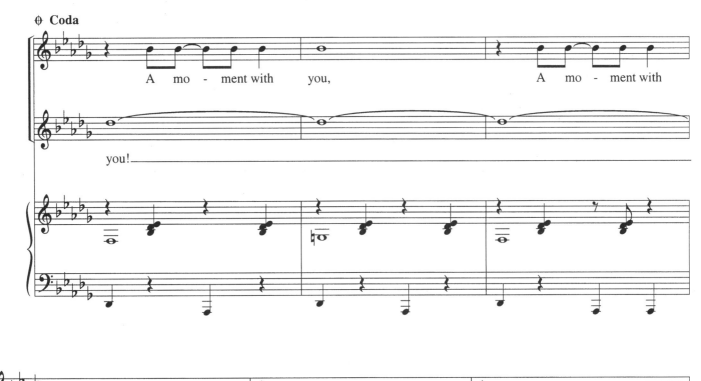

A mo - ment with you,

A mo - ment with

you!

you,

A mo - ment with...

A mo - ment with...

Record:

A mo - ment with...

A mo - ment with you!

Montana Chem.

from the Musical **SATURDAY NIGHT**

Music and Lyrics by
STEPHEN SONDHEIM

Gene says, "We're in a boom— To - mor - row, zoom right off of the graph!"

Artie:

U. S. Steel is up three points, Con-

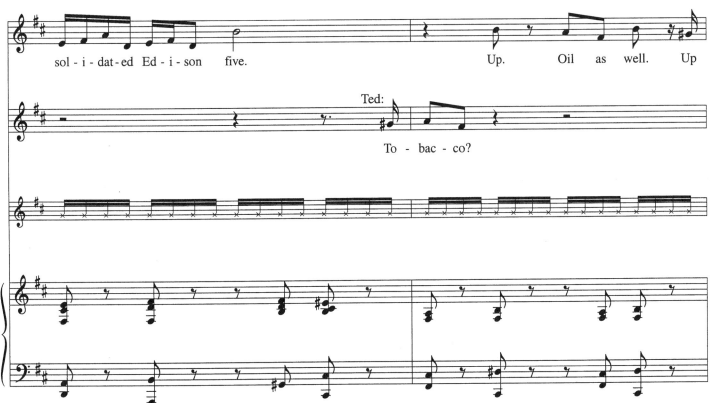

sol - i - dat - ed Ed - i - son five.

Ted:

To - bac - co?

Up. Oil as well. Up

four and sev-en-eighths for Tel. and Tel. Mon-tan-a Chem. ... Mon-tan-a Chem. ...

Mon - tan - a Chem.?

Both:

fell. But Gene says the mar-ket's med - i - o - cre, Gene says to-mor-row's a cinch.

mp *mf*

Gene says he heard it from some jok-er Who's the neph-ew of a brok-er Down at Mer - rill Lynch.

mp

All:
Corn went up, Wheat went up. Ev-'ry-thing that's list-ed on the street went up. Mon-

tan - a Chem. did not go up, But it did-n't go down! And Gene says, to-mor-row it-'ll take the town.

Artie:
First time!

dim. poco a poco

—— The stock is go-ing out of sight.——— Just wait un-til to-mor-row night.———

(Ticker Tape)

Artie, Ray, Dino:
Wait un - til to - mor - row...   Gene says,   wait un - til to - mor - row...

Hank, Ted:
Wait un - til to - mor - row...   Gene   says, wait un - til to - mor - row...

p

So Many People

from the Musical **SATURDAY NIGHT**

Music and Lyrics by
STEPHEN SONDHEIM

man _____ Who had-n't an - y, _____ With-out a pen - ny _____

mp

_____ To his name. _____ I had to go and

fall _____ For so much less than _____ What I had

planned from all _____ the mag-a-zines. _____ I should be

mf

my love for you._____ So man-y peo-ple laugh At what they don't know-- Well,

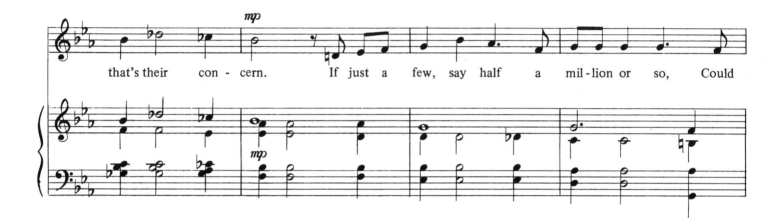

that's their con-cern. If just a few, say half a mil-lion or so, Could

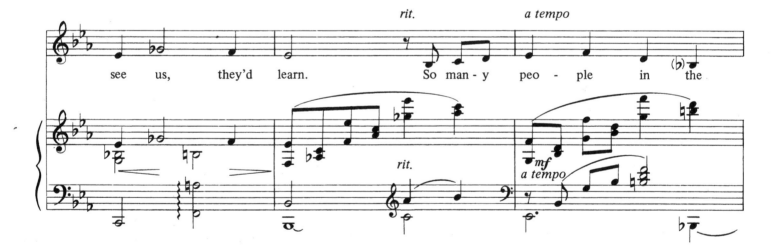

see us, they'd learn. So man-y peo-ple in the

world Don't know what they've missed._____ They'd

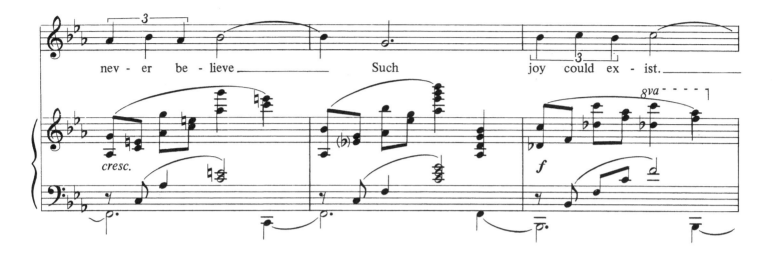

nev - er be - lieve_____ Such joy could ex - ist._____

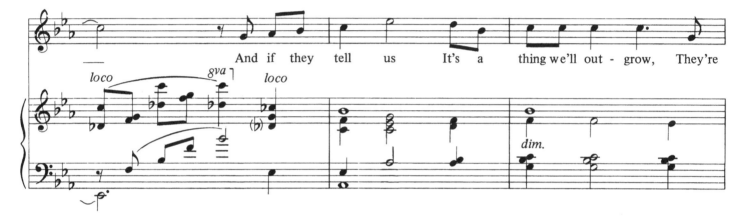

And if they tell us It's a thing we'll out - grow, They're

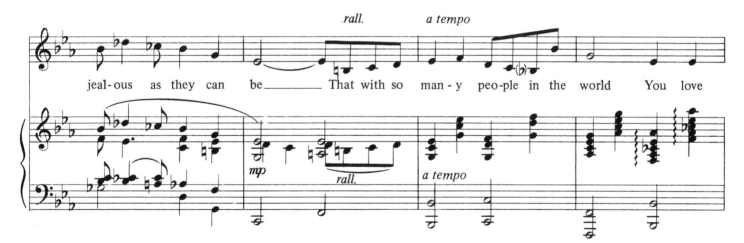

jeal-ous as they can be_____ That with so man - y peo-ple in the world You love

me!_____

One Wonderful Day

from the Musical **SATURDAY NIGHT**

Music and Lyrics by
STEPHEN SONDHEIM

All:
Hel-en and Gene are gon-na get mar-ried, Gon-na get mar-ried, Gon-na get mar-ried.

Hel-en and Gene are gon-na get mar-ried, Is-n't it won-der-ful?

Brightly ♩=64
Celeste:
One_____ won-der-ful day,_____ Won-der-ful

mf

things can hap-pen in a won-der-ful way!_____ Won-der-ful

girl meets won-der-ful boy._____ What a won-der-ful

chance to start a life____ Full of won-der and joy!_____

One_____ won-der-ful day,_____ Some-bod-y

won-der-ful sweeps all your wor-ries a-way!_____ If the

feel - ing's mu - tu - al, Then the fu - ture will Burst in - to song,___ And it's

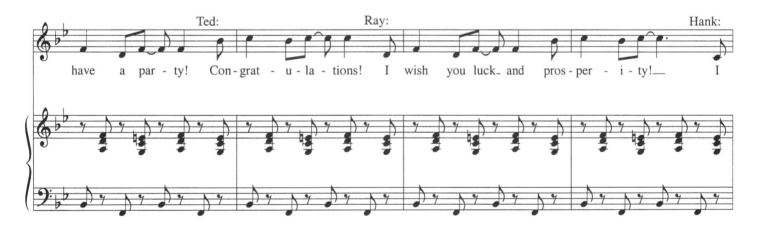

Slightly faster

Artie:

one won - der - ful day all year long! Let's

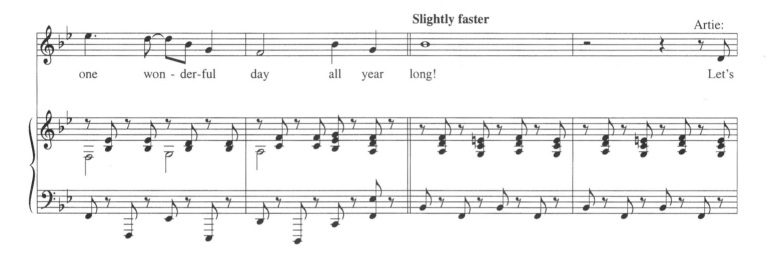

Ted: Ray: Hank:

have a par - ty! Con - grat - u - la - tions! I wish you luck_ and pros - per - i - ty!___ I

Flo:

wish you heart - y fe - li - ci - ta - tions! I wish that some - one would mar - ry me.___

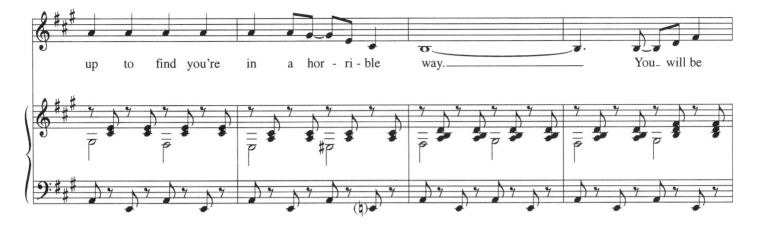

up to find you're in a hor-ri-ble way._____ You will be

mar - ried, You will be caught!_____ Ev - 'ry day you'll come

home and she'll be there.__ What a hor-ri-ble thought!_____

One_____ night on a swing_____ May-make a

cas - u - al af - fair a per - ma - nent thing._____ If you

can't keep cas - u - al, Then she has_ you all read - y to hook__ And it's one hor - ri - ble

Slightly faster

day— I can't look! My mar - ried dame

says, "It's a shame, But sex, if it's law - ful, Is aw - ful - ly tame." Hus - bands I've known

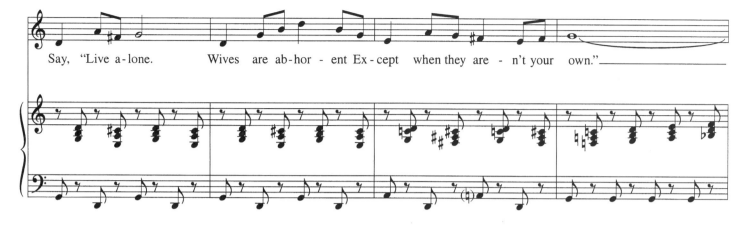

Say, "Live a-lone. Wives are ab-hor - ent Ex-cept when they are - n't your own."_____

Celeste:

_____ Pay no at - ten - tion To Mis - ter Smart - y, He's

full of beans and ba - na - na oil.__ He'll throw a wrench in This

love - ly par - ty, So just ig - nore__ him, Don't let him spoil this

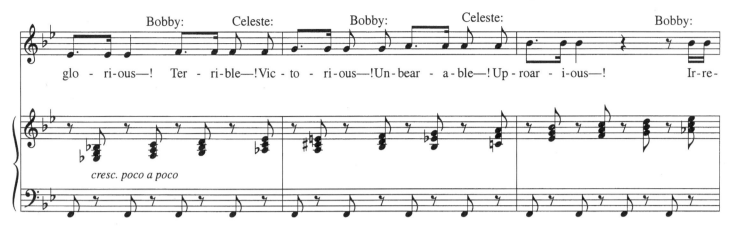

glo - ri-ous—! Ter - ri-ble—!Vic -to - ri-ous—!Un-bear - a-ble—!Up - roar - i-ous—! Ir-re-

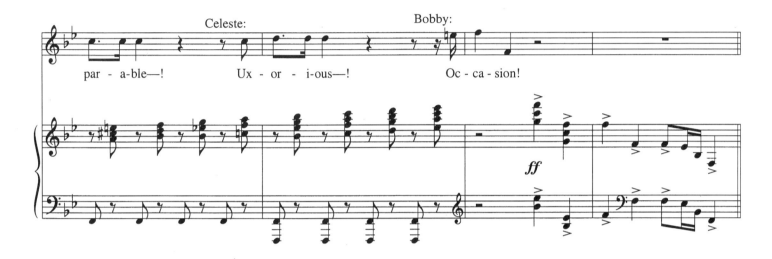

par - a-ble—! Ux - or - i-ous—! Oc - ca - sion!

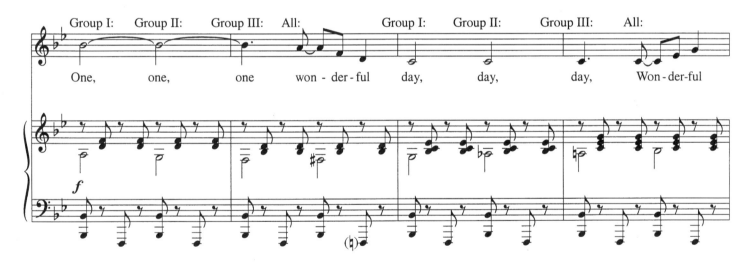

One, one, one won - der - ful day, day, day, Won - der - ful

things can hap - pen in a won - der - ful way._____ Won - der - ful

feel - ing's mu - tu - al, Then the fu - ture will burst in - to song,___ And it's

one won - der - ful day, One mar - vel - ous day,

sub. **mp**   *cresc. poco a poco al fine*

One beau - ti - ful day, One glo - ri - ous day,

One won - der - ful day   All year

long!___

I Remember That

from the Musical **SATURDAY NIGHT**

Music and Lyrics by
STEPHEN SONDHEIM

Ruminatively, rubato ♩=56

Hank:

I have a mem-o-ry for small de-tails. I have a mem-o-ry that nev-er fails.

I can re-mem-ber names, dates and pla-ces And ev-en fa-ces of peo-ple whose fa-ces I

don't want to know. I know the date of the Par-the-non, But there's a date that I'm

haz - y on: That was the date we had, I re-mem - ber, in ear - ly Sep-tem - ber, Or

was it No-vem - ber, three years a - go? Up to a cer - tain point my mind is

rit.

clear._____ Ev - 'ry de-tail of that date that fate - ful

rit.

Even rhythm

year._____ I ar-rived at sev - en;

Celeste:

Up to a point your mind is clear, no doubt._____ But I can re-mem-ber some

things that you left out._____ I was dressed at

sev - en, But you ar-rived at eight. And you were nev - er

late a - gain.___ I re-mem-ber that. Since you'd bought me

cof - fee All ov - er my new dress. From then on I con -

fess I for - get What I said and where I was at! But I

a tempo
did fall in love with you, I re-mem-ber I did fall in love with you, That's the one thing I

do re-mem - ber, I re-mem - ber that.

All For You

from the Musical **SATURDAY NIGHT**

Music and Lyrics by
STEPHEN SONDHEIM

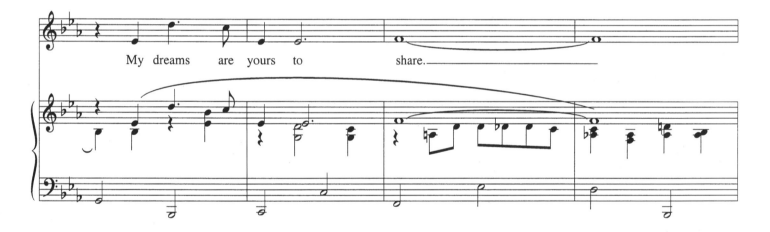

But that's be-cause I care.

If I get mad When I think you're wrong,

May-be I am wrong, too.

But good or bad, Ev-'ry-thing I do

Is all for love of you.

That Kind Of A Neighborhood

from the Musical **SATURDAY NIGHT**

Music and Lyrics by
STEPHEN SONDHEIM

All of us are for each and ev - 'ry oth - er hood, Oth - er hood.

All of us are for hoods.

It's that kind of a

neigh - bor - hood,_____ That kind of a neigh - bor - hood!_____

Freely and reverently
in Chorale fashion

Fair Brook-lyn, Pride of the Port of New York!_____ There's a

friend-ly golf course with greens_____ And a friend-ly hash-house with

beans._____ There's a friend-ly clink whence Come ju-ve-nile de-lin-quents, But

they were born in Queens!_____ Fair Brook-lyn!

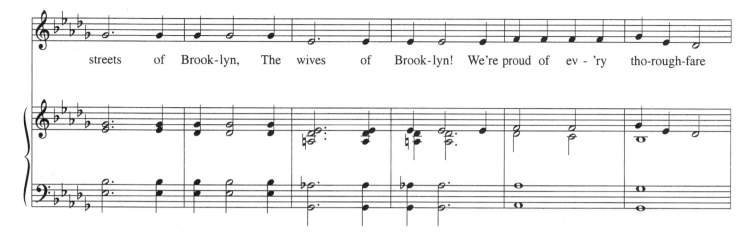

streets of Brook-lyn, The wives of Brook-lyn! We're proud of ev - 'ry tho-rough-fare

In this bo-rough, Fair Brook-lyn, The pride of, The thorn in the side of New

Tempo I

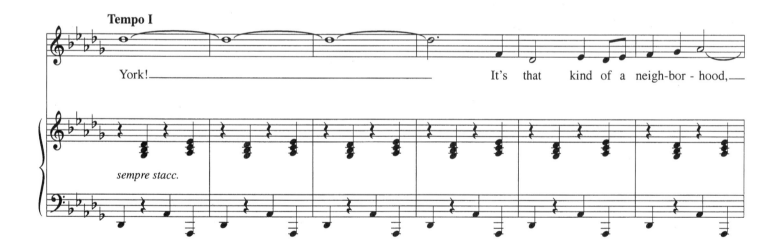

York!_____ It's that kind of a neigh-bor - hood,___

sempre stacc.

_____ Our kind of a neigh-bor - hood,_____

We're proud of our neigh-bor-hood

Ev-en if the world does-n't ap-prove!

And be - sides, Who can af-ford to

move?

What More Do I Need?

from the Musical **SATURDAY NIGHT**

Music and Lyrics by
STEPHEN SONDHEIM

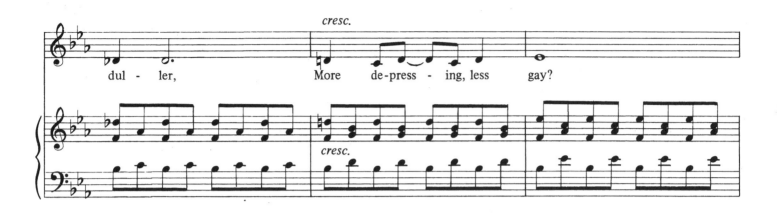

cresc.

dul - ler, More de-press - ing, less gay?

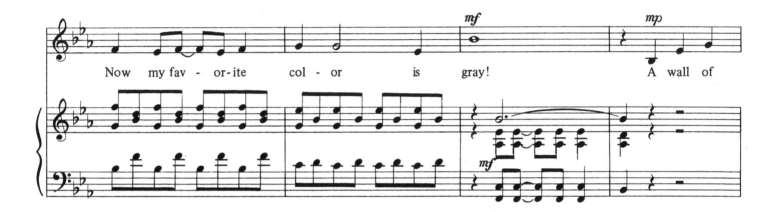

Now my fav - or-ite col - or is gray! A wall of

Più mosso

rain as it turns to sleet, The lack of sun on a one - way street; I love the

grime all the time, And what more do I need?____ My win - dow

pane may not give much light, But I see you, So the view is bright. If I can

love you, __ I'll pay the dirt no heed! _____ With

your love, __ What more do __ I need?

Some-one's shout - ing for qui - et, Some-one's start - ing a brawl.

Down the block __ there's a ri - ot, _____ And I'll buy it

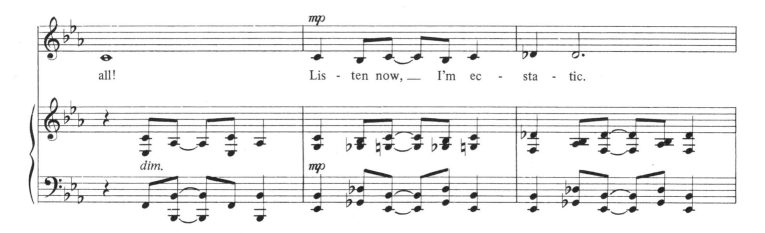

all! Lis - ten now, __ I'm ec - sta - tic.

Hold me close __ and be still. Hear the love - ly pneu - mat - ic

drill! _____ A sub - way train thun-ders through the

Bronx, A tax - i horn on the corn - er honks, But I a-

dore ev - 'ry roar, And what more do I need?___ I hear a

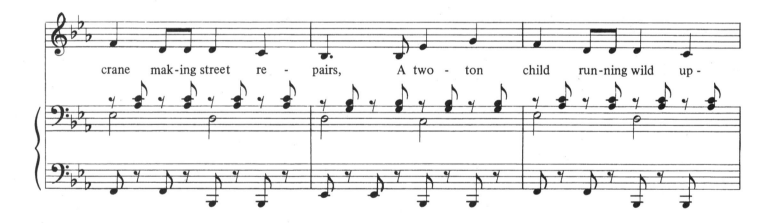

crane mak-ing street re - pairs, A two - ton child run-ning wild up-

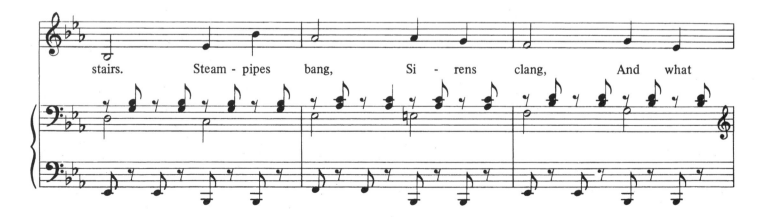

stairs. Steam - pipes bang, Si - rens clang, And what

more do I need? The neigh-bors yell ___ in the

sum-mer, The land-lord yells ___ in the fall, So

loud I can't ___ hear the plumb-er pound the wall! ___ An aer-o-

plane roars a-cross the bay, But I can hear you as clear as

day. You said you love me a - bove the sound and

speed! With your love, what more do I

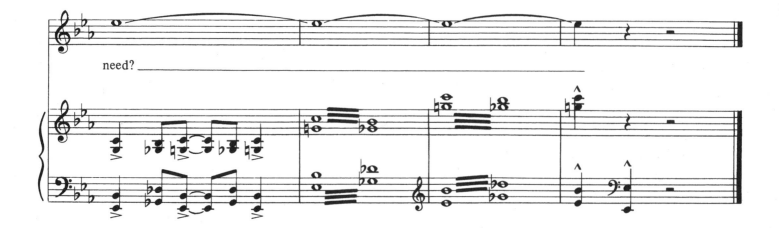

need?